" T A L K

The 7C's of Decision Making

David R. Reid

ECS
MINISTRIES
The Word to the World

Group study questions available at:
www.ecsministries.org

The Seven C's of Decision Making
David R. Reid

Dr. David Reid, a faculty member at Emmaus Bible College for 28 years, is the founder of Growing Christian Ministries. Information about his ministry and his teaching material may be found at www.growingchristians.org.

First Printing: 2005

Copyright © 2005 ECS Ministries

ISBN 1-59387-049-3

Published by:

  ECS Ministries
  P.O. Box 1028
  Dubuque, IA   52004-1028
  www.ecsministries.org

Cover: Ragont Design, Barrington, Illinois

Printed in the United States of America

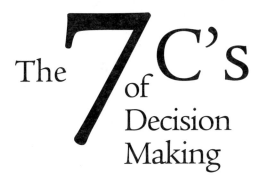

The 7 C's of Decision Making

> *"For I know the plans I have for you," declares the LORD, "plans to prosper you and not to harm you, plans to give you hope and a future."*
> JEREMIAH 29:11 (NIV)

*T*he term *seven seas* is used to describe the main bodies of water throughout the world. To say that a person has sailed the seven seas means literally that the person has navigated all the seas of planet earth. Many times, however, the term is used figuratively to refer to a person who has traveled widely and now has a wealth of experience.

The term *seven C's* has no connection whatsoever with the term *seven seas*. It is only a play on words and a mnemonic device to help us remember the means God uses to guide us in making decisions in life. If we extend this figure of speech, we could say that just as a person who has sailed the seven seas knows how to navigate the oceans of the world, so the Christian who has used *The Seven C's of Decision Making* knows how to navigate the sea of life.

Navigating the sea of life should not be viewed as a "hit or miss" decision-making adventure for the Christian. While the Christian life can be adventuresome and exciting, it should not be a hope-for-the-best, luck-of-the-draw, or shot-in-the-dark string of decisions. Rather, every decision can be made with confidence, knowing that God is in control of the ship. Although every person's life consists of the sum total of innumerable big and small decisions, Christians can be sure that when they come to God in faith and confidently ask Him for wisdom to make the right decisions, God will help them (see James 1:5-6). And although we may make some bad decisions along the way, we should not conclude that mistakes will cause us to be permanently cast adrift on the sea of life. When we realize and acknowledge our mistakes, God will provide navigational aids to properly change course.

> *Whether you turn to the right or to the left, your ears will hear a voice behind you, saying, "This is the way; walk in it."* ISAIAH 30:21 (NIV)

This Scripture is just one of many promises God has given us in His Word. It assures us that when we encounter issues that require us to make a decision, the Lord will direct us which way to go: "This is the way; walk in it." In the context of Isaiah 30, this promise is specifically directed to the nation of Israel, but the promise can certainly be applied to Christians today. The Holy Spirit lives in us, and God has promised, *"I will never leave you nor forsake you"* (Hebrews 13:5).

We can be assured that the Lord will guide us whether to "turn left" or to "turn right" when it comes to decision-making! And although we may not literally hear the voice of the Lord speaking behind us, we can be certain that

God will not abandon us when it comes to the important decisions we must make on the sea of life.

The seven C's are the means God uses to show us which way to turn in the decision-making process. We could call them navigational helps or aids for plotting our course and making course corrections. There is no "sacred sequence" to the seven C's; they are all important in the decision-making process.

The 7C's

COMMUNICATION

*C*ommunication is by far the most important of the seven C's. The primary way that God communicates with us is through His Word, and the primary way we communicate with God is through prayer. Scripture not only contains the navigational charts that help guide us along the way, but it also guards and supports the other C's.

When it comes to making decisions, most of what we need to know is obvious from the words of Scripture. Questions like whether or not to lie on a job application, whether or not to marry a Christian, whether or not to care for our aging parents, and whether or not to have family devotions don't require an in-depth, decision-making process. Why? Because answers to these decisions are easily found in the words of Scripture.

When the time comes for us to decide *which* job applications we should fill out, or *who* is the right Christian for us to marry, or *what* is the most efficient and compassionate way to care for our aging parents, or *how* to have the most effective family devotions, the Bible provides basic *principles* or *guidelines* that we can learn from and follow. While the answer may not be clearly stated in Scripture, the biblical guidelines (many of which can be found even in the narrative portions of Scripture) can direct us in to the right decisions.

For example, the biblical guidelines found in Deuteronomy 6:7 and Hebrews 10:24-25 clearly indicate that you should not apply for a job which would prevent you from fulfilling your family and church responsibilities. If you are single and have a strong conviction that God wants you to serve Him as a missionary in another land, a potential spouse should share your burden for foreign missions. If he or she does not, then you should re-evaluate your relationship with that person; consider the guidelines of Genesis 2:18 and Amos 3:3. The monetary amount of a future inheritance should not be a major factor in deciding the quality of care for your grandmother in her final years. Mark 7:8-13 and Ephesians 6:2 are useful guidelines. And a decision to gear your family devotions only for your own adult interests and not to meet the needs of your children would not be made if the guidelines in Ephesians 6:4 and Deuteronomy 4:9 are followed. The more biblical guidelines for making decisions you *know* and put into *practice*, the more obvious your course of action will be.

> The more biblical guidelines for making decisions you know, the more obvious your course of action.

Needless to say, prayer is absolutely vital in making decisions. First Peter 5:7 says, *"casting all your care upon Him, for He cares for you."* Does this care include concern about making the right decisions? Of course it does.

> God has promised us repeatedly in Scripture that He cares about our well-being.

Because God has promised us repeatedly in Scripture that He cares about our well-being, He will certainly answer our prayer for guidance in decision making, whether it concerns jobs, colleges, careers, homes, churches, marriages, families, ministries, finances, or anything else. But He wants us to pray!

Some people say that because God knows everything, He doesn't need us to pray and seek His help. This type of thinking is entirely wrong. Even though God knows all about us and the decisions we should make, He still wants us to communicate our thoughts and feelings. He wants us to express our dependence on Him in making these decisions. Good parents know what's best for their child, but they still want that particular child to communicate his or her desires and need for help. Similarly, God wants us to communicate with Him about our decisions.

In addition to this vital C of communication, God uses the rest of the seven C's to provide further directional or navigational help on the sea of life. In fact, consulting the other C's is necessary because any one C by itself— including the Scriptures—can be misused. Because of our sinful nature, we have the tendency to make the Bible confirm just about any decision *we* want to make! However, when all the C's are taken into account, our misuse of the Bible is held in check. The same is true when any of the other C's are mishandled.

The 7C's
CONVICTIONS

*T*he inner *Convictions* of the Holy Spirit, another important C of decision-making, must be closely examined. Because the Holy Spirit lives in every believer, Christians will have these convictions—and these promptings from the Holy Spirit will always be in line with God's will. They are therefore crucial when it comes to making proper decisions (see John 14:26; 16:13; 1 John 2:27).

> Convictions of the Holy Spirit must always be carefully examined to insure against self-delusion.

The problem, of course, is confusing the convictions of the Holy Spirit with the cravings of our sinful nature. Too often we convince ourselves that God is leading us to make certain decisions when in reality our personal desires are the primary influence. How many times has the expression "The Lord told me" been used to mask the reality of "I told the Lord"! Convictions of the Holy Spirit must always be carefully examined in the light of all the seven C's to insure against self-delusion.

The 7C's

COMMON SENSE

*A*lthough *Common Sense* is a C that we generally take for granted, it is definitely a means that God has given us to make decisions. In fact, most decisions in life are small and are made primarily on the basis of common sense. God does not want Christians to stop using sound judgment. Do you think He wants us to waste a lot of time and spiritual energy praying about which particular pair of shoes to wear, or whether or not to brush our teeth? Of course not! We must simply use common sense!

Even little decisions, however, matter to an omniscient God. After all, major events are sometimes influenced by the smallest decisions in life. And although God knows all the factors and variables of our lives, He expects us to use common sense in small matters such as brushing our teeth.

> Although God knows all the factors of our lives, He expects us to use common sense in small matters.

We must allow God to fit these small decisions into the overall pattern of our lives. He has blessed us with common sense, and it is our responsibility to use it for wise decision making about common, everyday matters. "Sanctified common sense" is part of the navigational system that God has given us.

The **7C'S** COMPOSITION

*H*ow God made us is what the C of *Composition* is all about. The way in which God sovereignly put us together, including our desires, personality, appearance, mental capacity, abilities, and spiritual gifts, is actually a means that God uses to guide us. For example, would the Lord guide you to become a singer or a pianist for His glory if He hasn't blessed you with natural singing or musical ability? Probably not! Notice the word "skillfully" in Psalm 33:3. *"Sing to Him a new song; play skillfully with a shout of joy."*

> "You are the body of Christ, and members individually."
> 1 CORINTHIANS 12:27

However, God may be guiding you to say "yes" to becoming involved in youth ministry if you enjoy kids and have a natural ability to relate to and communicate with children or teenagers. First Peter 4:10 is an excellent reminder to us all:

> *As each one has received a gift, minister it to one another, as good stewards of the manifold grace of God.*

On the sea of life, God can best use His tugboats, yachts, oil tankers, fishing boats, and aircraft carriers when they're willing to do the job they were *designed* to do!

The 7C'S
COUNSEL

*T*he *Counsel* of other believers is another of the seven C's that God uses in helping us make decisions. Proverbs 11:14 says, *". . . in the multitude of counselors there is safety."* Although the context of this verse concerns decisions affecting a nation, personal decision making is certainly an application. Mature, godly Christians can point us in the right direction and help us make right decisions. It is important to notice that help is assured through the counsel of *many* advisors. There is always a danger that a lone advisor, even a professional Christian counselor, may have a biased opinion about the situation. As a result you may be given a bad "compass reading" and end up off course.

The key for helpful counsel in decision making is to consult a number of godly men and women who have experience in navigating the area where you need to make a decision. These people are like channel markers—they point out dangerous hazards that might obstruct or hinder our way. This is how the body of Christ should work, and it is a primary way God guides us in making decisions. Just as different muscles and bones help your hand to move, so the different members of the body of Christ function as facilitators for one another.

> The key for helpful counsel is to consult a number of godly men and women.

The 7C's
CIRCUMSTANCES

*C*ircumstances* are obviously another one of the seven C's of God's guidance system. If you believe that God is sovereign, all-knowing, all-powerful and every-where at the same time, is there *any* situation or circumstance that is beyond His control? Of course not! *Nothing* happens by mere chance, and this includes *every* last detail of our lives. If our all-wise and loving heavenly Father is completely sovereign, can He not control circumstances to help us make right decisions? Of course He can! And at times He does send just the right winds across the sea of life to nudge our ship into the anchorage that is best for each one of us.

Those proverbial open and closed doors that believers talk about really do exist! They are not just a naive Christian view of circumstances, but rather a working definition of one of the C's that God has given to help us. But we must be careful about making decisions based *only* on circumstances. What looks at first like a closed door may actually be a door waiting to be knocked on and opened Matthew 7:7 says:

> *Ask, and it will be given to you; seek, and you will find; knock, and it will be opened to you.*

Proper discernment is of utmost importance in evaluating circumstances. An apparently open door may not really be open. A job offer with a higher salary does

> We must be careful about making decisions based *only* on circumstances.

not necessarily mean that God is directing us to move to a new location; we may have forced our own interpretation on that circumstance!

It is even possible for Satan to manipulate circumstances. This would certainly be part of his scheming strategy to blow us off course (see 2 Corinthians 2:11 and 11:14). So prayerfully analyze your circumstances. God definitely uses those circumstances in His navigational system. The proper use of the other C's will safeguard us from reading too much or too little into the C of circumstances.

The 7 C's

CONTROL

*F*inally, there are times when God steps in and takes *Control* of the decision-making process in no uncertain terms. In some situations there is no question that God is indicating the decision He wants us to make. A model train operator normally monitors the movement of the model train by the use of remote controls. Sometimes, however, the operator reaches into the layout and moves or straightens out a boxcar or an engine with "hands on" control. In the same way, God sometimes reaches in and takes control of our situation in such a way that we are no longer even involved in the decision!

In the normal decision-making process, for example, a good offer on our house may or may not be an indication that God wants us to move. But if we get no offers at all, it may indicate that God is controlling the situation and is preventing the move. This illustrates that sometimes the Lord takes the decision-making process completely out of our hands. When we are suddenly removed from one ministry and find ourselves in the midst of a new ministry, without having made any decisions ourselves, it is probably a good indication that God is guiding us by control.

Sometimes God steps in and controls a decision because the other C's seem to be pointing us in a direction that is not actually what God desires for us. For example, God used the C of control in the life of the apostle Paul in Acts 16:6-10 (the Macedonian vision). At others times God controls a decision because He knows of some impending danger or a future unlikely turn of events that a common sense decision-making approach would miss completely. Other times, God just graciously chooses to use the C of control to deliver us from the dilemma of doubt in the decision-making process.

CONCLUSION

*T*he sea of life can be turbulent at times, with numerous hazards and obstacles to avoid. Knowing and using God's navigational system of the seven C's helps the growing Christian in making good decisions that avoid disaster and directs him in following God's will for his life. Proverbs 3:5-6 is an excellent reminder:

> *Trust in the LORD with all your heart, and lean not on your own understanding; in all your ways acknowledge Him, and He shall direct your paths.*

THE SEVEN C'S OF DECISION MAKING

- ➤ COMMUNICATION
- ➤ CONVICTION
- ➤ COMMON SENSE
- ➤ COMPOSITION
- ➤ COUNSEL
- ➤ CIRCUMSTANCES
- ➤ CONTROL

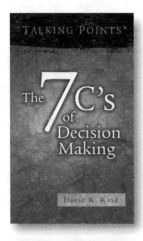

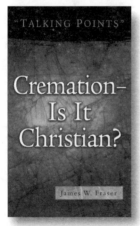